Spot the Difference

Eyes

Daniel Nunn

Heinemann Library
Chicago, Illinois

Customer Service   888–454–2279

Visit our website at www.heinemannlibrary.com

Photo research by Erica Newbery
Designed by Jo Hinton-Malivoire
Printed and bound in China by South China Printing Company
10 09 08 07 06
10 9 8 7 6 5 4 3 2 1

Library of Congress Cataloging-in-Publication Data
Nunn, Daniel.
  Eyes / Daniel Nunn.
      p. cm. — (Spot the difference)
  Includes bibliographical references and index.
  ISBN 1-4034-8474-0 (hc) — ISBN 1-4034-8479-1 (pb)
  1. Eye—Juvenile literature. I. Title. II. Series.
  QL949.N86 2007
  591.4′4—dc22

                              2006007240

Acknowledgments
The author and publisher are grateful to the following for permission to reproduce copyright material:
Alamy pp. **4** (Nature Picture Library), **15** (Guillen Photography), **16** (NaturePicks), **17** (Steve Bloom Images); Ardea pp. **6** (Chris Harvey), **8** (Jean Michel Labat), **12** (John Daniels), **14** (Ferrero-Labat), **19** (John Daniels); Corbis p. **21** (O'Brien Productions); FLPA p. **7** (Minden Pictures/JH Editorial/Cyril Ruoso); Getty Images p. **10** Digital Vision; Nature Picture Library pp. **5** (Bruce Davidson), **9** (Meul/ARCO), **11** (John Downer), **13** (Phil Savoie), **18** (Georgette Douwma); Science Photo Library p. **20** (Mark Thomas).

Cover image of a tiger's eyes reproduced with permission of Steve Bloom.

Every effort has been made to contact copyright holders of any material reproduced in this book.
Any omissions will be rectified in subsequent printings if notice is given to the publisher.

Contents

What Are Eyes?. 4

Where Are Eyes Found? 6

Different Shapes and Sizes. . . . 10

Amazing Eyes 16

Eyes and You. 20

Spot the Difference! 22

Picture Glossary. 23

Index 24

What Are Eyes?

eye

Many animals have eyes.

Animals use their eyes to see.

Where Are Eyes Found?

Most animals have eyes on their head.

This is a gorilla.
It has eyes at the front of its head.

This is a zebra.
It has eyes at the
sides of its head.

This is an earthworm.
It has no eyes at all.

Different Shapes and Sizes

Eyes come in many shapes.
Eyes come in many sizes.

This is an owl.
It has big eyes.

This is a mole.
It has small eyes.

This is a frog.
It has bulging eyes.

This is a leopard.
It has shiny eyes.

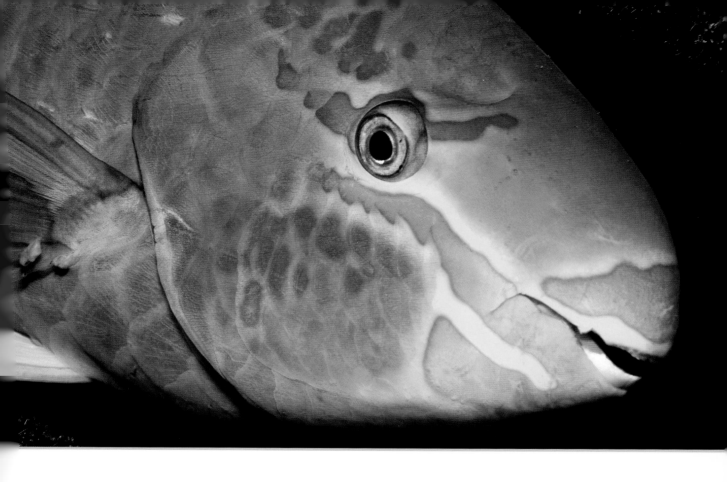

This is a fish.
It has bright yellow eyes.

Amazing Eyes

This is a bee. It has two big eyes.
It also has three little eyes.

This is an eagle.
It can see very far.

stalk

This is a crab.
It has eyes on the end of stalks.

This is a chameleon.
It can look in two places at one time.

Eyes and You

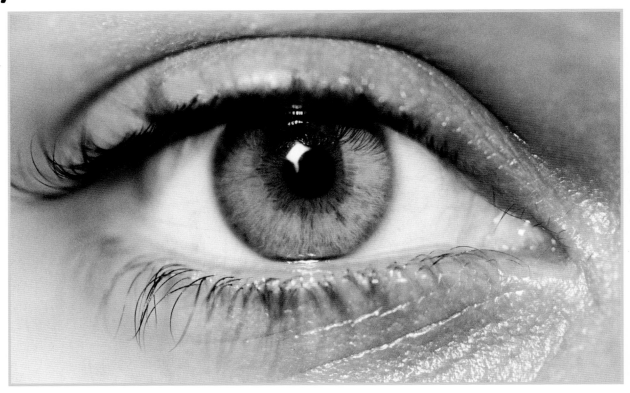

People have eyes, too.

People use their eyes to see.
People are like other animals.

Spot the Difference!

How many differences can you see?

Picture Glossary

bright full of color

bulging something that sticks out

stalk long, thin body part of some animals

Index

bee, 16

chameleon, 19

crab, 18

eagle, 17

earthworm, 9

fish, 15

frog, 13

gorilla, 7

leopard, 14

mole, 12

owl, 11

zebra, 8

Note to Parents and Teachers

National science standards recommend that young children understand that animals have different parts that serve distinct functions. In *Eyes*, children are introduced to eyes and how they are used to see. The text and photographs allow children to recognize and compare how eyes can be alike and different across a diverse group of animals, including humans.

The text has been carefully chosen with the advice of a literacy expert to enable beginning readers' success while reading independently or with moderate support. An animal expert was consulted to provide both interesting and accurate content.

You can support children's nonfiction literacy skills by helping them to use the table of contents, headings, picture glossary, and index.